For Bernd who taught me brevity

And Yvette who helped me understand it and him

Contents

Thanks to Thoreau! 4
Late Autumn Feast 5
Feast 6
Someone else's feast 7
In Memory of a Daughter 8
Weeping 9
Evening 10
The Sikh 11
Tattoo 12
Fire 13
Waltzing above 14
Departure 15
Mother's Day 16
Trying to Escape 17
Dreams and Reality 18
Misguided 19
Recreation 20
Rich Statement 21
Joy de Vivre 22
Of hunger and greed 23
My Garden 24
End of a Marriage 25
Looking down 26
Letting go 27
ADD of the Aged 28
Change of heart 29
Sorry, Folks 30
The Thief 31
Priorities 32
Of Seniors 33

Never Ever 34
Sitting under a starlit sky, talking to a dead husband 35
Of saving 36
Cyberspace Communication 37
The Ageing Female Achiever 38
Loneliness is 39
Mother 40
Errare humanum est 41
Same, same 42
Advice 43
Artist's Advice 44
Learn to Tango 45
Terezin 1944 46
Florence 47
Kafele and the War for Democracy 48
Emergency surgery in Syria or any other place of No Hope 49
The Price 50
Farewell 51
Palliative Care 52
Common Apology 53
Making a poem 54
Dealing with memories 55
Looking 56
To a Traveller 57
For a Judoka 58
For Florence 59
Impress 60

Thanks to Thoreau!

As I turn pages,

Working through books of poems,

Poignant at times,

I despair.

Have we forgotten Thoreau?

Reading voluminous lyrics

(a brief reminder to myself)

Takes time.

Making a haiku

Quote -*will take a long while*- unquote

Do I have enough time?

Late Autumn Feast

Sparrows, finches dance

Around wheat ears, pick seeds.

Winter approaches.

Feast

Blackbird swings on branch

Rich with red elderberries

Worm tangling in mouth

Someone else's feast

Royal blue dragonfly

Flutters over murky pond-

Hungry green frog snaps

In Memory of a Daughter

For Sarah

Cells divided

Cells died and we died

With you

Weeping

Grey clouds

Hug mountain range

Drop, turn into tears

Evening

Soft mountain contours

Fade into the quiet night

City lights pop up

The Sikh

He wears a turban

Practices compassion

Cares

Tattoo

Lover devotion

Inked into once muscled arms

Shrivels, fades

Fire

Flames eat birch wood,

Burning, warming

Us

Waltzing above

Silent glider swings

Below, above, beyond clouds,

Dancing in the wind.

Departure

Isolated,

Blanketed by

Silver Clouds

Death calls. Life leaves.

Mother's Day

Fifty times

An empty mailbox

Creates silence

Trying to Escape

Fruit flies climb window

Climb, slide, fall. Climb, slide, fall.

Die in vain.

Dreams and Reality

Off the beaten path

The earthling dreams of sunshine.

When it burns, he dies.

Misguided

Young sparrow spreads wings,

Bangs into window pane-

Drops on cement floor, dies.

Recreation

Blackbird cleans feathers,

Sings on tin roof, calls

Mate to mate, creates

Rich Statement

We plan to help

Sick and poor refugees

Tomorrow.

Joy de Vivre

Emerald-green dragonfly

Sips dew from dandelion leaf-

Another good day!

Of hunger and greed

Mouth wide open

Hungry toad snaps flies

Chokes

My Garden

Young sparrows pick seeds.

Next week, no fresh lettuce-

But songs at sunrise

End of a Marriage

No fight

No Argument

Nothing

Looking down

Dark Mountain Range

Dotted with village lights

Sinks info sky

Letting go

I toss your ashes

Into the restless sea

Remembering for the umpteenth time

How you tugged me into your arms

While breaking my heart,

Piece by piece.

ADD of the Aged

Patience no longer a virtue,

I ignore Bestseller lists,

avoid historical horror or romance,

usually entangled.

I no longer allow

winding strings of aching words

or love-dripping, stinging stanzas

coughed up by inflamed, sore throats

in need of anti-inflammatories

to creep into grey matter,

however decayed.

Give me a Haiku!

My time is limited.

Change of heart

The rooster crowned,

observing his flock

Flew over the fence, released,

relieved, carefree.

Many feather losses later

he returned for another circle dance.

Surprise!

Mother hen did not respond,

Desires gone,

buried with baby chicks,

Sorry, Folks

If I could push a button, erasing letters, poems,
spoken words, songs, pasted together elegies,
tear pages out of year books,
wipe memory with Mister Proper,

slash life passages, sweep sentences
deep under Persian runners,
plunge bleeding verses deep into wells,
hide them under brush, let mold take over,
suffocate rhymes in sand dunes,

it would not change anything.

The Thief

If lyric can't feed

Wide mouths in yearning faces

Wilted bodies on cold beds

Desperate souls

Forget it,

The green, purple-hooded dwarf said,

Fetching paper and pen

Before he disappeared

Priorities

Our local paper puts news in perspective.

Page one:

Brussel votes for tax on plastic bags

Midpage with photo:

Edathy, once promising politician,

pays 5 grand to leave child porn case behind.

Last page: Rape of infant in India.

Of Seniors

Up in age,

We should give up dreams,

Close chapters,

Competing is out of the question.

Wrinkled faces and souls

Are denied entrance

To dances of discoveries.

Publishers have no plan

For aging newcomers,

Viewed dead before the event.

Never Ever

You have never been so present

Before.

When your face shines

Through loaded clouds

High above soaked meadows

I want to rip it down

Caress it,

Lock it

Into the ever so present.

Sitting under a starlit sky, talking to a dead husband

Hi, guy!

Hanging around Pluto,

Chasing Wagon or Bear

Fighting Mars,

Riding Venus?

Drop the guilt.

Enjoy!

Of saving

I am writing on

Your Ipad

The one

You left behind

After wiping

Dark and tender memories

saved

During lonely nights

I replaced them

With mine

Stored in a folder

For no one.

Cyberspace Communication

Louis LinkedIn.

Frieda followed.

Angelina M. who fucked

My man in 1998 Twittered,

Asking for Acceptance!

Xing offered a free sign in,

Sara Somebody wants to chat

And Mortimer, September Eleven Casualty,

Continues to follow my Research Gate updates

From Somewhere

While I am waiting

For the One, departed April 29, 2014,

To befriend me on Facebook.

It could happen.

The Ageing Female Achiever

After shutting down computers,

She acknowledged empty rooms,

Faced truth,

Regret.

Love had escaped early.

Success wooed her after stretches

Of lonely meals, cold beds, calls.

She wanted love,

Achieved meager fame.

Loneliness is

…sitting at a hotel bar

counting ceiling lights

and wine bottles neatly stacked

behind counters.

….mentally matching drink

and food to plain people,

watching them talk

or not.

…..envying the ugly man

stroking his fat wife's thigh,

imagining fingers wandering up

into the moist.

Mother

She

Often

Sat by

The bay

Window

Watching

Sitting still

Left forefinger

Rhythmically stroking

Lips. No background music

Interrupting silence

Kind stillness

In thoughts

Known

To her

Only

Errare humanum est

She had hoped barking dogs,

yelling kids,

dripping bathroom faucets,

her breathing,

rustling newspaper pages,

branches banging on windows,

firewood crashing into itself

and Garrett's fiddle

would only bother him

until he recovered.

He never did.

Same, same

Fish are slippery, all of them,

perch, dolphin, salmon, haddock,

sword- or catfish, whales, cod.

Can't hold them on a hook for long,

forget netting.

Even the decrepit slip through fingers,

jump into sewage lines,

never your aquarium.

Can't keep them, unless you cut, slice

or suffocate them.

Fish is fish.

Martha paused,

watching her man

slide through the gate

into the dark.

Advice

Bow when entering.

Souls forgive dualities

But echo what is.

Artist's Advice

Rays hidden behind

Mountains cannot paint petals.

Rise. Color the earth.

Learn to Tango

With your inner eye

Listen and accept imperfection.

Dance.

Terezin 1944

Strings hung up, wait.

Safeguarded from ash and snow,

Silence deafens.

Florence

Bereft of hope

I knocked on your door.

You read me Heine,

Served Israeli wine

taught Chutzpah

Who said Germans and Jews

Can't live in love?

Shalom.

Kafele and the War for Democracy

Old Kafele, crippled by pain, leaned over,
sagging shoulders shaking,
Covered his son's holed body with the torn flag
shaking.

After pushing the long bloody snake of a gut into
the smelly torn tomb,
He bends over to retch in the gutter, shaking.

Waving his stick, Kafele chases dogs from the
carousel of coffins,
All shaking.

Emergency surgery in Syria or any other place of No Hope

All day, she hands him scalpel, drill bits,

Clamps, retractors, lancets.

He reaches, cuts, dissects and staples,

Expecting losses.

Mothers in plastic sacks, forever deafened

Are stacked in corners.

Lost screams ride up high

Scaring away hungry dogs.

All day, she hands him scalpel, drill bits,

Clamps, retractors, lancets.

He reaches, cuts, dissects and staples,

Their shoes are soaked in blood.

At dawn, she hands him

Scalpel, drill bits, clamps, retractors, lancets

Ignoring orphans

Drowning in darkness.

The Price

No one,

Cried the hero's mother,

Has ever won a war.

And kept the medal

And the sorrow

And the death certificate.

Farewell

Allow me to hold your hands

to help you through the dark,

dense jungle of deep-rooted fears.

Drop armor,

leave combat and battle,

harm, hurt and injury

Allow me to weep

when I cradle your suffocating heart

your tender soul

Let me hold

the lantern,

guiding you into the thick cushion

of safe dreams

Palliative Care

We provide comfort.

Treatment will keep pain bearable,

Curative treatment is out of the question.

We provide physical assistance,

Institutional care, food for a dwindling frame,

Help carry emotional and spiritual matters.

Morphine will cloud

Grey matter with illusion,

Curative treatment is out of the question.

Common Apology

The snake after biting the rabbit:

You took one step to too many, my dear,
You should have known better,
But nevertheless, I am sorry.

Yet the wound was profound
And the poison effective.

Making a poem

I sit

and let the giddy bustle pass.

Harsh sirens and disturbing noises

fade with the colors and the voices.

I sit

and watch a string of words amass,

some vowels dance and blend

into free verse. Some sounds offend.

I sit,

let muffled melodies trespass,

some buzz around, most disappear

into a distant ecosphere.

I sit

alone in barren space,

when suddenly thin vapor

lifts, and rhymes march onto paper.

Dealing with memories

It's because

the muscled body passing

pushed memories of

satiated hunger,

salty sweat dripping,

And because

the Savignon Blanc hinted of

heated grounds, stinging nettles

and passion fruit,

I had two glasses,

large, full-bodied!

Looking

Standing on top

The mountain climber

Faced heaven and himself

To a Traveller

Thousand miles

Are painful for the unprepared

Take one step at a time.

For a Judoka

Resisting strong winds

Breaks mighty trees.

Bend with the wind

For Florence

Your Good Green Footstool

Blanketed by Carpets of Nanoparticles

Lost color and diversity

Impress

Production and Publishing:

BoD – Books on Demand, Norderstedt

ISBN 978-3-7392-2032-1

Copyright © 2015 E.Blaurock-Busch

All rights reserved. Without limiting the rights under copyright reserved above, no part of this publication may be reproduced, stored in or introduced into a retrieval system, or transmitted, in any form, or by any means (electronic, mechanical, photocopying, recording, or otherwise) without the prior written permission of both the copyright owner and the above publisher of this book.

Permission to photocopy or reproduce may be obtained from the author at ebb.blaurock@gmx.de or ebb@microtrace.de